T0209465

THE MAN WHO
CHEATED
DEATH

THE MAN WHO
CHEATED
DEATH

GUILFORD BARNES

WESTBOW
PRESS®
A DIVISION OF THOMAS NELSON
& ZONDERVAN

WestBow Press books may be ordered through booksellers or by contacting:

WestBow Press
A Division of Thomas Nelson & Zondervan
1663 Liberty Drive
Bloomington, IN 47403
www.westbowpress.com
1 (866) 928-1240

ISBN: 978-1-9736-7138-1 (sc)
ISBN: 978-1-9736-7139-8 (e)

Library of Congress Control Number: 2019911178

Print information available on the last page.

WestBow Press rev. date: 8/15/2019

GUESS IT ALL STARTED WHEN I WAS THREE YEARS OLD. I was playing on an old mule rake when I slipped, fell, and cut my leg. My mother came running out of the house and got me.

I said, "Mom, I see my liver."

She told me, "No, that's not your liver. You've just cut your leg." She put some black salve on the cut and then put a bandage on it.

The next Sunday, we went to church, and when we got home, we saw people gathering at the old Mill Hole.

Dad asked, "What's wrong?"

A man said, "Someone has drowned."

I was so scared as I watched them pull the man out of the water that I went running around the house to hide. My father sat me down, and he prayed for me because I was so upset. His prayer to God was to keep me safe all the days of my life, and this included that no bone in my body would ever be broken.

Uncle Rosier, my mother's brother, lived with us, and when he turned the right age, he was called into the army. That morning, my dad was to take him to the train station to catch the train to report for duty. Before he got into my dad's 1937 Chevy car, he hugged me and gave me a quarter. I thought I was rich.

He left, and we did not see him again for four years. He would write to us and let us know where he was and how he was doing. My dad would pray every day that God would bring him home safely. While my uncle was in the army, he was wounded but finally came back home to live with us. He would not talk a lot about the war. If he did or even tried, he would start to cry.

In 1941, my dad bought a farm in Sidney, North Carolina—better known as the Whiteville or Tabor City area—and it had a swamp that ran through it, Gum Swamp. That swamp still runs today. We moved there in December 1942, and it is still my home place today. The house had wood shingles, and there was no ceiling in it. At night, we could see the stars through the roof. I would see the chickens through the cracks in the floor. We burned wood in the two fireplaces to stay warm in late fall and winter.

My dad started working on the house, adding a ceiling and walls, in the spring of 1943. I would go fishing in the swamp and catch flyer bream. They sure were good. Mom would fry them on the wooden stove, and I would cut the wood into little pieces to burn in the stove. My daddy loved fish, and I loved to catch them then. I still do today.

My dad was a Baptist preacher, and he would pray for me and call my name out to the Lord to keep me safe all the days of my life. My dad was fifty-five years old when I was born, and my mom was twenty-four. Dad had been married twice before. With his first wife, he had three children, two boys and a girl. Sadly his wife died. He married again, and they had five children. This wife died as well. He later met my mom at church. They married, and I was their only child.

My dad adopted two of the children out to Oscar Wilson, Delia and Junior. Their grandmother raised Elisa and Marie. Dad kept George Robert with him. We called him Buster, and I loved him. Buster got sick with scarlet fever, and they gave him up to die. But Dad got down to pray that God would let him live, and he finally got well. So I guess that is where I learned how to pray and trust in God.

I was born on January 19, 1938. In 1944, I turned six years old. We had a milk cow, and I had to milk her before school each morning. I would get up at 5:00 a.m. to milk the cow by lantern light and be ready for school by 7:00 so I could catch the school bus. Dad bought me a calf and told me to let him suck one udder. If I could raise him, I could have him. I fed and raised him until he got big enough to eat grass. Then I would take a chain and stake him out to eat the grass in other areas.

Mom and Dad bought me an air rifle, and the next Sunday morning, I took my calf and staked him out near the ditch. I took my air rifle and went hunting for a while before church. I came back about an hour and a half later, and my calf was gone. I saw the chain and started looking for him. I followed the chain, and when I got to the ditch, I saw my calf with his head under the water. I couldn't get him out.

I fell to my knees and began to pray. I don't know how long I prayed, but some black people who lived on the farm heard me and came running down there. I told them my calf was in the ditch, and they got him out for me. He lay there for a while. Then he just got up. God heard my prayer, and I thanked Him for saving my calf's life. I grew and learned more about God.

One day I wanted a soft drink, and the store was about three hundred yards from our house. Dad gave me a nickel. As I was walking to the store, I was looking around me, and in the ditch about halfway to the store, I saw some pages torn out of a Bible. I reached down and got them. Dad had bought me a little pocketbook (a man's billfold), so I folded up the Bible pages and put them in my pocketbook. I told my dad about the pages, and he read them to me. It was about the prodigal son. He gave them back to me, and I put them in my pocketbook. I still have them today.

That summer, I was a drag boy while working in tobacco. My dad had bought me a mule. If you touched her back feet, she would kick bad. So we would undo the traces at the hames and back ban and slide them off her back.

One day, I was dragging tobacco, and the road had some stumps in it. I was making the mule trot. The drag hit a stump and threw me out between her back feet. She stopped the drag, and I crawled out from between her feet. She never moved. I sure was scared. I had cheated death for the first time by the grace of God, and I sure did thank Him.

The next year, Uncle Pete, Mom's baby brother, came to stay with us. He and Buster, my half-brother, were about the same age. They would pull tricks on me and on each other. They would turn the mules out and tell Mom and Dad that I did it so I would get a whipping. Boy, would they laugh!

So one day we had a corncob war. It had rained, and the cobs were soaking wet. I got a wet cob and threw it at my brother. It hit him in the face, and I got another whipping. My brother got some bamboo briars about three feet long. He took his knife, trimmed the ends where he put his hand to hold them, and slipped up on me. He grabbed me by the arm, and boy, did he put a whipping on me. Every time he would hit me, those briars would stick in my behind. I told him I would get him back.

The barn had hay in the top, and when I saw him at the top of the barn forking hay out for the mule, I slipped up behind him and pushed him out of the barn. When he fell to the ground, the pitchfork stuck him on the ground through his clothes, and I got my butt beat again. I never told what my brother did to me. I guess I always kept things bottled up inside.

As time went on, we would grow crops year after year until I was twelve. That year, my mother got sick and went to the hospital for a few days. My dad asked me to fix supper one of those nights, and I agreed. I don't remember what all I fixed that night, but I do recall one thing, the biscuits. I got the flour out and put in some water. I rolled them up just like I had seen Mom do. I patted them out and put them in a pan. I put them in the oven and kept looking at them. When they began to cook, they cracked open. Then

I thought they were done, so I took them out of the oven. They were as hard as bricks.

Dad asked, "Son, did you put any lard in them?"

"No."

He said, "No wonder they cracked open."

We had a big laugh and had supper from the other things I had cooked.

Buster joined the air force. Uncle Rosier got married, and Uncle Pete left to stay with Grandma. Then I was all alone with just Mom and Dad. Dad had bought a BAC tractor, and when it came time to plant another crop, I started to disc and plow the fields at twelve years old. I felt like the whole world was on my shoulders. After school I would plow until dark, and Mom would fix supper. She always had a drum of water outside where I could take a bath with warm water day after day.

I would get up before day, do all the chores, get ready for school, and fix the land to plant the crops. Finally my dad hired an attendant farmer, Guilford Coleman, to help me. He lasted one year and then left. I was all alone once again.

Dad hired another attendant farmer, Verland

Cribb, who lasted two years. The next year he hired Corby Ward. I sure did like him. He was smart, and he would get up early in the morning and go to work. We still cultivated the crop with mules. Dad traded the old BAC tractor and got a new one.

Two weeks later on a Sunday morning, he told me to go check the milk cow in the back pasture. She was going to have a calf any day now. I asked Dad if I could drive the tractor, and he said yes. My buddy who lived down the road came walking up, and he went with me. I drove down that good ole winding road and found that the cow was doing fine.

My buddy, Robert, said, "Let me drive back."

I agreed. He put it in high gear and gave it all the gas. Boy, we were moving. There were bad curves in the road, and he did not slow down around the first curve and lost control. The tractor ran into a tree and threw us off, ruining the tractor. I sure hated to come home and tell my dad. But I had cheated death again. I was all right but bruised up quite a bit, and thank God and by His grace, I was safe again.

Robert's dad and mother separated after we turned the tractor over. His mother, Lucille, moved to

Montgomery, Alabama, and his father, Hoyt, relocated to Richmond, Virginia. Robert and his sister went to live with their mother. Dad traded tractors again, this time getting a D-10-AC. Boy, it was nice.

It was time to start another crop. I had grown up and begun to look at the girls more. My friend Wilber Spivey came to the house on a Saturday night with his dad's truck and two girls.

He asked, "Do you want to go to the Plaza drive-in just down the road?"

"Yeah, but let me see if Dad will let me drive his truck so we will have more room."

I went into the house. "Dad, could I drive the truck?"

"No, you don't have a driver's license."

"Please!"

"No."

"I'm going to drive it anyway."

He got up and beat the fire out of me. That was the first time he had ever whipped me. I finally got away from him, so we all went to the show in Wilber's truck. That night, my dad had a stroke on his left side, so they took him to the hospital.

I felt so bad. I sure did love him. I thought I was the cause of it. After about three days, they called from the hospital and said they had done all they could do. If we wanted to see him alive, we had better come right away.

I told my mother and aunt to go ahead. They drove my aunt's car. I said I would take the truck and come up later. I went inside the house, got down on my knees, and began to pray.

"Lord, I am but a boy. I have no one else to lead me and guide me with wisdom." I was crying. "Lord, let him live until I become a man."

And the crying stopped. I felt a relief come over me, and I got up, took the truck, and went to the hospital where he was. When I got to his room, Dad was sitting on the bed, smoking a cigarette. He not only lived until I became a man, but he also saw my first child. God had answered my prayer.

We brought him home and fixed a bed in the room where the heater was so he would stay warm. I kept that heater going. That next Saturday evening about 3:00 p.m., a car pulled up, and it was Uncle Pete and Uncle Rosier. They were quarreling, and

Uncle Rosier came inside. They were cursing at one another.

I had a .22 rifle standing in the corner of the room, and Uncle Rosier grabbed it. I got up when he opened the door. Uncle Rosier cocked the rifle and threw it on Pete. I grabbed the rifle just as it went off, pushing the barrel up. It shot just over Uncle Pete's head. I pushed the door to lock it, and they were still cussing and raising sand.

Uncle Pete came to the window, and Uncle Rosier grabbed a brick from under the heater and threw it at Uncle Pete, but it went through the window and hit him on the head. There was a bush in the yard, and under it was a pile of bottles. Uncle Pete started throwing bottles through the window, and one almost hit my dad.

I took Dad into the bedroom and hid him under the bed. I told him to stay there until I cleaned up the mess. I had a shotgun in my room, and I went and got it because I was going to kill Uncle Pete.

When I came back in the room where the heater was, he was still throwing bottles through the window. I threw the gun on him, and Uncle

Rosier grabbed it. We tussled over the gun, and it went off.

I still had the gun and began to load it and shoot again. Everybody began to scatter. My mother slipped out the back door and got Uncle Pete in the truck and left with him. I don't know where Uncle Rosier got to. There I was with the windows broken out. It was cold and getting dark.

I got Dad out from under the bed and began to try closing up the hole to try to stay warm. After a while, Mom came back home, and we had to make do with the windows till Monday. We bought new windows and put them in.

The next weekend, Uncle Pete got in a fight on Horseshoe Road with AC Coleman. He cut him up bad, even cutting his heel strings into his bare feet, rolled him into a ditch, and walked away. The man that ran the store called the law, and they took AC to the hospital. The doctor sewed him up the best he could. He lived but couldn't ever walk again like he should.

Uncle Pete ran through the woods into the Big Bay where Uncle Homer lived, and Pete got one of

Uncle Homer's mules, rode the animal back down to our house, and hid from the law. They looked for him with bloodhounds, but he had evaded the bloodhounds by riding the mules back. He stayed hid out behind our house in Gum Swamp in a tobacco drag, where he slept. He would work in the fields during the day, and we would carry him food and water to where he slept.

After about six months, Sheriff Pridgen came to me and wanted to talk with me. "I know that you know where Pete is. I know you, and there will be a lot of trouble if the law comes in here to look for him. If you will, talk him into giving himself up and call me. Then I will come by myself and get him. That way no one will get hurt."

So I talked Uncle Pete into giving himself up. The sheriff came on a Saturday night, and Uncle Pete gave himself up. Uncle Pete was then tried and sentenced to five years in prison.

When the winter was over and spring began, we boys at school wanted to go to the Azalea Festival in Wilmington, North Carolina. My friend Jason had a 1950 Ford convertible. We were going to leave early Saturday morning, but Mom and Dad said I couldn't go.

Charlie Ward, Herman Goodman, Ernie Royals, and Slick Cartrette went on earlier in the morning. At about 9:00 a.m., I was out watering the cows and the mule. They wrecked not long after they left. Someone—I believe it was one of the teachers that went as a chaperone—called from the scene of the wreck. She was behind them. The gas tank exploded and set them and the car on fire. They all died except for Slick. He was messed up bad, and his life was never the same.

She said, "I sure am glad that Guilford didn't go."

There again, I cheated death for the third time by the grace of God. God's hand was surely on my life.

Spring had begun. Corby and I began to plant another crop. I had quit school so I had more time to work on the farm. I was strong and healthy. We would work from daylight till dark. With God's blessing, we made a fine crop and kept it clean.

After we gathered the tobacco and sold it, Lonzie Ward, Corby's brother, would sometimes help, and all his children would assist too. Lonzie asked if I wanted to go with him to roof a warehouse in Boone, North Carolina, for Rossie Coleman.

I asked, "Corby, would you get the corn in the barn for me?"

He said, "I will. Go on ahead. I will look after things."

I told Mom and Dad that I was going to Boone to work with Lonzie. Dad, who was getting better, told me to go ahead and to be careful. He loved me so much and said he would pray for me every day.

We got there and went straight to work. I slept on a hardwood bench in the warehouse office to save the money I was making, seventy-five cents an hour, to be exact. We would work from daylight till dark. I ate canned food and pork chops every day. We had a two-burner stove to heat our food on. I wrote Mom and Dad, letting them know that I was saving my money to buy myself a car.

We came home on a weekend the last of November, and I gave Mom over five hundred dollars. I told her to go buy me a car. We went back up there to finish the job.

We got back home just before Christmas. Uncle

Rosier had moved into one of the tenant houses on the farm. Mom had bought me a black 1950 Ford for $450. I felt like a king. But after driving it for about two weeks, it started to run hot. Somebody had messed it up. The heads were cracked. I was a sick man, but my friend JB Coker had come home from Milwaukee for Christmas.

He asked, "Would you like to go back with me? There's plenty of work up there."

I said, "Yes, I can go and work with you until the spring. Can Uncle Rosier go?

He agreed. Then I asked Uncle Rosier, who said he would work until the spring.

We got up there and got a job at Glone Tannery working with cowhides. Man, that place smelled bad.

My dad gave me a hundred dollars before we left. He said, "You put this in your pocketbook, and if you haven't found a job when your money runs out, you buy a bus ticket and come home."

Thank goodness we were making a dollar per hour. It cost us twelve dollars per week in room and board. We stayed in the Carving Faircloth boarding house. I would send my money home. I asked Mom to trade and get another car, and she did. It was a blue 1954 Pontiac.

I told her it was an old woman's car, but I drove it anyway. I was out driving around, and I saw Carolyn Soles out in her yard. I had known her for many years, but she had filled out and looked good. She was fifteen, and I was almost eighteen.

I started going to see her every evening. It was only three hundred yards from our house. We got married that fall after the fall crop was gathered. One day we were sitting around at my mother's house, and Robert drove up in a nice, green and white 1956 Ford. He said that his mother's husband had bought it for him. Lucille had gotten married again to a man whose last name was Woodrow.

I told him, "Carolyn and I are going to Florida to work through the winter."

He asked, "Can I go? We can drive my car."

I agreed, so we all went to Orlando in his car. I got a job with Dixie Lily Distributors Company. We would deliver groceries to the stores. I was a helper. Jim Craddock was my boss. Robert got a job stocking shelves with one of the grocery stores in Orlando. I rented a house, and we all stayed together.

After about a month, Robert left and went back to Montgomery to live with his mother. I told Jim Craddock that I needed a car to travel back and forth for work. He went with me, and we found a 1946 Ford. When spring came, I told Jim that I was going home to plant another crop.

He hated to see me go. He told me, "You are a good worker."

I said, "I have to go."

He asked, "Do you think that old car will make the trip?"

"I'll leave it beside the road and catch the bus if it doesn't."

I kept putting oil in it every fifty to seventy-five miles. I told Carolyn if we make it across the Charleston Bridge, we were home free. We made it home on a Sunday morning. Mom and Dad were glad to see us. I checked the oil in the car and could not find any, not a drop. Thank God we were home.

We stayed with Mom and Dad for a while. We planted another crop. Uncle Garland, now married, moved into one of the small tenant houses. Some had two rooms; others had three. We were working close to one hundred acres of land with one tractor and three mules. Carolyn gave birth in the winter to our son, Jeffery Kim Barnes. We stayed home that winter, and Uncle Garland, Corby, and I cut wood and sold it to get money to live on.

The next spring, Carolyn and I moved into a little house that Dad had built on the edge of the woods. It had two rooms. We made another crop that upcoming spring. That fall, Dad hired Corby and me to build another tobacco barn. So we built it and roofed it.

Dad said, "Son, you did a great job. Why don't you start in the roofing business?"

I thought about it for a bit and decided to go for it. We had all the work we could do. We farmed and roofed for two years. We'd get off work, stop at the beer joint, and drink several beers before we came home.

Carolyn began to say that I was seeing another woman.

I said, "No, we're tired. I just drink some beer before we come home."

Uncle Rosier had moved out of the big house. It had running water, a bathroom, three bedrooms, a kitchen, and a hallway. So we moved in. It was nice. We kept farming and roofing. Dad didn't get out much anymore. He just sat around the house.

We were setting out tobacco in the spring. I looked down the farm road and saw someone coming down the road toward us. Uncle Pete had gotten out of prison. He jumped in and went right to work. He stayed with Mom and Dad, and we made a fine crop that year. I gave him my old 1947 Ford. He would drive it every weekend to see Grandma.

Almost three weeks later, Uncle Herman, my mother's brother, got in a fight with Mr. Hayes over his wife and him having an affair. Herman beat the man badly, and the man told him he was going to kill him on Saturday evening.

Sunday morning, Herman was in the house with Mr. Hayes' wife. When Mr. Hayes looked through the window, Uncle Herman shot him right between the eyes with a .22 pistol. The bullet didn't go through his head. It went around it, so it didn't kill him. Mr. Hayes had a shotgun, and he shot Uncle Herman in the back, killing him instantly. We buried Herman on Wednesday.

The next weekend, Uncle Pete drove back to see Grandma. He had a flat tire and didn't have a spare. So he left his car at a house next to Grandma's that Uncle Guilford had built. Some black people were living in the place.

The next weekend, I bought a new tire on Saturday. I took Uncle Pete down to change the tire.

I told him, "I'm going over to see some girls I know. I'll be back in a little bit."

I stayed gone about three hours. When I got back, the law was leaving with an ambulance.

I pulled up and asked, "What happened?"

The lady said, "There was a big fight. Pete and my husband had been drinking moonshine."

Uncle Carl, who lived next door, had called the law. Deputy John Coleman lived down the road and had another deputy with him, Thurman Butler. Pete had his knife out and was going to cut the black man. John shot Uncle Pete in the chest three times. My mother's people were very malicious at times and could be dangerous, harmful people.

I went to the hospital to see him that Saturday evening. I came home on Sunday morning and went back to see him. I walked up to the side of his bed.

He looked up at me and said, "Guilford, we won't ever work hard together anymore." He was hugging the pillow.

I watched him die. It was the hardest thing to see. We buried him on Wednesday of that week. I thought about it all week. I don't know why I left him and stayed gone so long. If I had been there, they probably would have killed me too because I loved him. We kind of grew up together. He was five years older than I was. We slept together, played together, and loved each other so very much.

Corby and I went back to work patching houses, covering houses, and doing farm work. I drove Dad's truck everywhere we went. Mom drove my 1954 Pontiac. It was so ugly, and I didn't want to drive it anyway. We were making plenty of money and still drinking beer after we got off work. We would stop at a bar and drink for an hour or more. When I got home, Carolyn started questioning me.

We got in a quarrel, she slapped me, and I smacked

her back. That night she had gotten a gun from her stepdad, and while I was sleeping, she told different people she had put a gun to my temple. But Kim got in the way. She didn't pull the trigger. That was on a Friday night.

On Saturday, I went to town and bought me a hat that had a red feather stuck in it. I was looking at it in the bathroom mirror. She came in the hallway and shot me in the stomach. I jumped in the bedroom, where I had a .22 rifle. I shut the door and started looking for my rifle. I couldn't find it anywhere. It was right there the night before. I looked under the mattress, in the closet, and all four corners of the room. It was gone. I normally kept it in the closet in the corner so Kim wouldn't mess with it.

I knew then that she had it and she planned to kill me when I came back from town. I stood there for a minute or two, trying to figure out how I was going to get out of this room alive. There was a front porch and a window near it with a blind. I rattled the blind like I was going out the window, and I heard her go out on the porch.

I opened the door and stepped down the hall. I

just knew she was going to shoot me in the back. The truck was parked at the back door. Most of the time it would whine before it would crank, but this time it started right up. She came running down the hall and out the door with the gun. I was driving away. I cheated death again by the grace of God.

I drove to my neighbor's house. "I've been shot. Can you drive me to the hospital?"

He told me yes, and when we got there, they took me straight to the emergency room. I was burning like fire.

The doctor checked me out and said, "You're a lucky man. The bullet is lodged in your side."

He cut out the bullet, a .22, and gave it to me. He put a bandage on me, and I went home.

I told my neighbor, Woodrow Hardee, that I was going to kill her. I went back to the house, and she was gone. I started looking for my rifle. I found it between the mattresses. She had put it back. I had plenty of bullets in my dresser drawer. She had walked out to the store where her mother was. She was pregnant again, about four months along.

When I pulled out the yard, I saw her walking

down the road. I pulled in at my mom's yard and got out with my gun.

Mom asked, "What are you going to do?" She didn't know that I had been shot.

"I am going to kill Carolyn."

"What for?"

At that time, I still had not told her Carolyn had shot me, so I said, "She shot me."

"Are you all right?"

"Yes." I went around the house and got behind a tree.

My mom hollered at her, "He is going to shoot you!"

Carolyn picked up Kim and put him in front of her. I didn't shoot at her because I didn't want to kill my boy. Soon after that she went and talked to Judge Al Williams, who told her that she needed to get out of this part of the country.

"I know them people. My mother is related to them. He will do what he said. I've known him from his youth, and he will do what he says."

Carolyn went to Kansas City, Missouri, to stay with some of her people. While there, she had a baby girl, whom she named her Bridget Yvonne Barnes.

She kept in touch with her mother, Kit Harrelson, who lived at Sidney, three hundred yards down the road.

I kept seeing Kit every now and then, and she told me that Carolyn had met up with some man and moved somewhere in Texas. By that time, the hate had worn off.

Corby and I kept roofing, and our name spread all around from town to town, even to the local beaches. I told Corby I was going to get a contractor's license and start doing contract jobs. I named the business Barnes Roofing Contractors. I got my ID number and license. Corby said he would work for me just by the hour, and I agreed.

My dad was getting feeble, and he made out his will. Each child would get so much. Some of the boys began to ask about the will. I didn't say anything to anyone.

One of the boys said he would be glad when the old man died so he could get his part. One of the others told Dad about it, and boy, did he get mad. So Mom and Dad went and got a lawyer. He gave me everything. Mom got lifetime rights on it all.

I told Mom and Dad that I would work the farm one more year. I was going full time with my roofing business. After that year, they passed a bill that you could sell your tobacco pounds to someone else if you wanted to. I told Mom to sell and said she could have the money. We had lots of pounds. We sold it to my friend CW Todd for three dollars per pound. Mom got several thousand dollars from the sale.

I fenced off the farm and started buying cattle. At this point, I was staying by myself. I would go out on the porch at night and pray. "Lord, I know there is someone out there that is a good person."

I dated many girls for a while. One Sunday I was out driving around and passed by the house of my friend Fred Spivey. I saw this girl outside in the yard, and something told me she was the one.

On Monday I started asking around, trying to find out her name. I used to eat supper at the Starlight drive-in in Whiteville, North Carolina. The waitress there was familiar with lots of local ladies, and I had known her for quite some time because I had eaten there a lot.

I told her, "I've seen a young lady walking in the yard at Sidney that I'm kind of interested in."

"Where at?"

"Fred Spivey's yard."

"That's my friend Barbara. She lives in the old white house down from the store at Sidney."

"Yes, that's where I saw her in the yard."

She gave me Barbara's phone number. I called her and told her who I was. She said she could meet me in Whiteville. I drove up there the next weekend, and we got acquainted. I began to see her one to two times a week.

Aunt Sudie left her husband and moved in with Mom and Dad. She had a little boy, Mickey. I got attached to him and loved him. I treated him like he was my son. Aunt Sudie began to date a man, Gillie Mower.

Mom told me one day, "Let Sudie move into your house, and you can come and stay with your dad and me."

I agreed.

Dad called me in his bedroom one night after work and said, "Guilford, I won't be here much longer. I want you to go pay off the people I owe." He gave me three names.

"Sure, Dad, I will do that."

"I don't want anybody to look in my casket and say, 'That man died owing me.'"

So I went and paid all his debts off. Not much later, probably four months, he died.

But before he passed, he called me back into his room. "Son, you have a bad temper. Try to control it. Whatever happens in your life, you may fall many times, but keep praying and never ever turn loose the hand of God."

I had joined the National Guard unit some time before Dad died, and we had weekend drills.

Captain Smith said to us, "All you new recruits that have joined this past year, you have to go take sixteen weeks of basic training."

I said, "Lord, there goes my business."

I came back and told Corby and Mom.

Corby said, "I'll take care of things."

Mom told me, "I'll answer the phone and take down names and addresses to jobs."

"I will try to call in every day if possible. I will call

my contractors and let them know that you are taking care of things till I get back."

I told Barbara I would write to her every week, and I did. After eight weeks in Fort Jackson, South Carolina, we got our paperwork of where we were going. They sent me and several others in the outfit to Fort Pope, Louisiana, for eight more weeks of training.

Everything was fine at home. Corby was taking care of the business; Mom was writing checks and paying the labor and the bills as they came in. We got on a plane in Columbia, South Carolina, and flew into Alexandria, Louisiana. Several taxi drivers took us to a hotel in Alexandria.

The next day they came to get us on a bus from the base. The bus driver told us the plane that we had come in on had crashed after takeoff and killed everyone on it. By the grace of God, I had cheated death again, for the fifth time. I remembered my dad's prayer to keep me safe all the days of my life.

I will never forget that place. It's the only place I've ever been where you could stand in mud up to your knees and sand would blow in your eyes. There was a town outside of the base called Leesville, and every other building was a tavern. I've never seen so many pretty girls in one place in all my life. Every time we would get a weekend pass, we would head to Leesville.

Finally after eight weeks in Fort Pope, I came home and got up with my friend KC. We went out on the town on Saturday night. We went to Else Ward's tavern on the South Carolina line. I had traded cars and left it home during basic training. It was a 1956 black-and-white Pontiac.

After drinking till about 11:00 p.m., we headed home. We started racing with this guy on the way home. I lost control of the car on a curve, and the last time I looked at the speedometer, we were going 110 miles per hour. We went out on the curve, scrubbed the side of a big oak tree, went through a cornfield, and headed straight back to the edge of the road.

The guy we were racing with came back and said, "Part of the time, the headlights were shining straight up."

He had a chain in his car and pulled me onto the road. We drove to KC's home, which was not very far away. We got out, cleaned up, and went to bed. The next morning, his mother was about to kill us. She called us a bunch of drunks.

That Sunday morning, the guy we were racing with came over to see us. His last name was Richardson. We drove back down to the cornfield and the big oak tree. We had sideswiped the tree, and that is when I got really scared. If we had hit the tree, both of us would have been killed. I had cheated death once again, for the sixth time.

I kept on talking to Barbara, and we talked about getting married. In the spring, there was a very large hailstorm in Lumberton, North Carolina. I had hired Barbara's brother, Mitchell, to help. I got a call from the town of Lumberton. It was some insurance company, and they wanted to know if I had wanted to bid on some jobs. Of course I said yes.

I drove up and met the adjuster. We drove around town, and I had never seen so many damaged houses in my life. The hail and wind had taken its toll on this town. We drew up the contract.

They asked, "How many crews can you get?"

"I could get two right away."

I took Corby and a crew and started to work the next week. The first job was a schoolhouse. We put crews on it. They wanted to get it first. I trained Mitchell to handle jobs, and I left him in charge of things at home and around the beaches.

I rented a trailer house for us to live in. I was making so much money that I didn't know what to do with it. I bought a new truck and car. Then I started buying all the land around home. God really blessed me. We worked from daylight until dark, seven days a week.

After several weeks, I came home. Barbara and I went to the drive-in. We didn't see much of the show. We talked, and I told her everything about me from my womanizing to my habits. I told her I probably would not ever change. I told her she couldn't tell me what to do, where to go, or when to come back. I would never go through that again in my life after what I had been through in my previous marriage. My mother would try to tell me something to do, and sometimes I would listen, but not always.

I told Barbara that I had a chance to buy ten acres of land in Kissimmee, Florida, and Mom told me not to. Aunt Sudie's boyfriend owned it. He would take ten thousand dollars for it. Mom said no. I knew it was a good buy. I knew the land, and I had seen it while working with Dixie Lilly. Jim Cradock and I had looked at the land before. JG Moore bought it. It was prime land. I didn't have the money then.

I told her about my whole life. I said, "If you want to get married, you think about it until I come back home again. There is one thing you will have with me, and that is a good life. I will never beat on you or try to control you. I will never leave you. You have to promise me that you won't steal from me or look in my pocketbook."

I took her home. The next day, I went back to Lumberton to work. Mitchell was doing a good job. I left without talking with him about work. I stayed gone for several more weeks. I returned home and picked up Barbara.

We went back to the Starlight drive-in. I asked her, "What's your answer?"

"I'll marry you."

So we set a date and got married. I told Aunt Sudie that I needed the house and my wife and I were going to move in. She got mad, but she moved out, and we moved in.

About two or three weeks later, on a Sunday after dinner, I was walking out in the yard. Aunt Sudie and JG Moore pulled in the yard. She got out of the car and was cursing and yelling at me. Barbara and Uncle Garland were in the house. She opened her purse, pulled out a pistol, and started shooting at me.

I felt the bullet go through my hair. I ran my hands over my scalp. The bullet had grazed my scalp. I was bleeding a little. I pulled out my pistol, and we had a shootout. Both of us were running. We were shooting at one another until we ran out of bullets.

I ran in the house to get my shotgun. I was going to kill her. JG got her in the car, and they left. I had cheated death for the seventh time.

I asked Barbara if she wanted to go with me, and she asked me where we were going. I told her that I was going to hunt down Sudie and kill her. She said she would go with me.

I got my gun, and she got in the car. We drove everywhere that I thought Sudie would be. I thank God that I didn't find her. I didn't see her for about six months. Then one day I came home from work, and I stopped to see Mom. And there was Sudie. We forgave one another and started a new life.

Uncle Garland moved out of the house they lived in, and Aunt Sudie moved in it. Mickey would stay with her and with me some. Finally after he finished school, he wanted to go see his dad, who lived in Baltimore. He stayed gone for about three years, and then one day he came home. He had gotten married and had a son. He moved into a house in Fair Bluff, North Carolina, for a while.

One day he came to me and said he wanted to move back home, but all the houses on the farm were filled up. I told him that I would try to get a trailer set up for him behind my house. I did, and he moved in it and went to work for me. He was so happy. Each day his little boy would come to see me for a while.

One day when I came home, Barbara met me at the door. She said, "You won't believe who's here."

"Who?"

"Kim."

I was so glad to see him. He had grown up to be such a fine boy. I had not seen him in five years.

He said, "Dad, can I stay with you? I don't want to stay with Mama anymore."

"Yes."

He had come in on the bus. So he and Barbara unpacked his things, and we gave him a bedroom. He was so happy. We signed him up for school at Williams Township. The roofing business was doing great. Corby and Mitchell were handling the jobs. By that time, I started another business big time, cattle. I was buying baby beef calves for Greenwood Packing Company and cows for Whiteville Packing Company. I had bought a new truck just to transport cattle.

I asked Mickey if he would like to learn how to buy cattle and transport them from place to place. He agreed, so I started letting him go with me so I could train him and show him what to buy.

About three months in, he was doing great, so I turned him loose. He would come in late at night, get a few hours of sleep, and head back on the road early in the morning. God was so good to me. Barbara was the secretary at an oil company in town and had been there for several years. I had built a new office building. I told her to give them a quit-work notice. I wanted her to come work for me.

She was pregnant then with our first child. She was the best secretary you could find. Corby and Mitchell would turn in all the bills and labor for the roofing business, and she would write out all the checks. It sure did help take a load off Mama and me. Mickey would turn in all the bills from the stock yard, and Barbara kept all that paperwork in order and mailed out all the checks. I put a bid on the consolidated schools for the roof work in Brunswick County and won all three jobs.

I was talking to a man about hunting in a neighboring county. I had never killed a deer before. He said I could join their hunting club if I wanted to. He was from the area and was also working on the school job. So I joined the hunting club. The club had an end-of-year oyster roast so all the men and their wives could go and fellowship with each other.

Barbara and I went to the oyster roast. We got through eating, and I walked outside. There were others outside to fellowship with, and we all had a really nice time. We were able to get to know each other better.

My new hunting buddy told me where to sit in the wooded area for best results in shooting a deer. After about twenty minutes, a truck pulled up about sixty yards from me. My buddy got out with his gun. We both saw a very large buck that was headed in his direction. He took a shot at it. The only problem was that it was too close to me.

I took cover, and he missed the deer. I don't think he realized how close he actually was to me. I hit the ground. He jumped back in his truck and left.

I got up and said, "Lord, I thank you for sparing my life for the eighth time." I had cheated death again.

I got in my truck, and I left. I later found 236 acres of woodland near home, and I bought it to hunt on. Several hundred acres surrounded it, one way in and one way out.

I decided to start another business, where I would auction off farm machinery. I started buying tractors and equipment. I set up a yard of about five acres right in front of the office.

Barbara had a baby girl, whom we named Robin. I

had built a shop and hired an older man as a mechanic. He worked about four months and quit. One night we were eating supper, and I heard a knock on the door. I went out to see who it was. It was a man that everyone called Shorty.

Drunk, he had run into the ditch in our driveway. He asked me, "Can you pull me out?"

So I did. The next day he came to see me. I had heard that he drank quite a bit. He said he wanted to work for me. I told him that I didn't need a drunk in my business. He said he would quit drinking. I asked him what he could do and told him if he were going to work for me, I would not put him on the payroll. Instead I would pay him a hundred dollars per week. I was hoping he would say no, but he said he would take it and he would show me what he could do. I told him to be at the office at 7:00 a.m. on Monday.

He came to work on time, and I showed him what to do.

I told him, "Be here at seven o'clock every morning. Barbara would open the office and the shop if I weren't here. I would call every day to see how things were going."

About a month later, I got up with KC about a cow sale. He asked if I would ride with him to Saluda, South Carolina, to the stockyard. I agreed, so we met early the next morning.

After we got there, I started talking to Johnny Shore, an old friend of mine. He ran Shore Livestock Sales. I told him that Mickey worked for me, and he said he knew him and that Mickey was a good judge in livestock. I informed him that I knew he was because I had trained him.

I asked Johnny if he would let Mickey buy some yearlings for him. We worked most of the sales in North Carolina that he didn't. I told him we would put things together and bring them to him Wednesday of each week, sale day in Saluda. He said he would try me and see how it goes. I had picked up another customer, and Mickey was happy.

The business was growing. After the sale ended, KC and I rode out to see his friend. We met out in his cow barn. They were unloading cows, and one got loose and got in a big canal ditch. It was dry weather with no water in the ditch.

The man asked me to take KC's truck and go

around to the next road to cut her off. It wasn't very far. I didn't know that part of the country. The cow was at the end of the ditch, so I put the truck in park and left the lights on.

I jumped out to turn the cow around, and there was a barbwire fence. I was trying to get through it, and I got stuck. I saw some headlights over the hill, and I was parked on the wrong side of the road. The car was moving at a high rate of speed. He was trying not to hit the truck. He didn't see me and was heading straight toward me.

I said, "Lord, this is it."

When it was about four feet from me, a giant force from God stopped it dead still.

The man got out and said, "I can't believe it stopped so fast."

I had cheated death for the ninth time. I recalled my dad's prayer again, that God would take care of me all the days of my life and that not one bone in my body would ever be broken. I told KC about it on our way home. I began to think about it, about how God had blessed me. I had accepted Jesus as my Savior when I was very young but had strayed away so far from God. Like the old song "Coming Home," I said, "I am going to head home."

I began to pray more. I had a long way to go. Sometimes you must put your feet in motion with prayer. Barbara got pregnant again, and all the businesses were doing great. Shorty had come a long way. God was indeed blessing me.

Then one day, my old friend Robert drove up in his car, and he asked if I would go with him to Virginia. We used to go a lot of places together.

I said, "No, Robert, I can't go. I have too much going on with work."

The next day his dad called me and told me that Robert had passed away. Jerry Garrell, my dear friend from childhood, and I drove to Virginia for the funeral. Robert and I had shared some amazing times together as children and young men, but now my friend was gone. I came back home to my family and my businesses. I was very sad for my friend. But I had to walk on in life as usual.

Barbara and I loved the mountains. I told Barbara that I was going to the mountains to look for a place to get away on the weekends. She instructed me to get a pretty place. I agreed. I left on a Wednesday, and I stayed in Asheville that night. I got up the next morning and started looking around. I looked all day for a pretty place that we would love.

That evening I came up on a little town called Marshall. I saw a sign that said "Brook Reality." I pulled over, parked, got out, and walked across the street. An older man was standing on the sidewalk. I introduced myself. His name was CP Brooks.

I told him, "I'm looking for a place to buy so my family and I can get away on the weekend."

He said, "Meet me at the café down the street at eight o'clock Friday morning. I will show you what I have available."

I met him, and we rode all day looking. I didn't see anything I liked. He told me that he had one more place, a big piece of land, available that was on the French Broad River. He said there was a lady who was interested and he had to check and see if she had bought it yet. He told me he would go with me to look at it the next morning.

We drove to the top of the mountain, and I saw the old house and a big barn. This was a big place, close to a thousand acres. CP told me the previous owner had died and left it to his heirs, who were scattered all over the country, with the closest one being in Florida. They all had signed to sell. There was two and a half miles of riverfront on the French Broad River. You could see the rim of the trees. It was so far away that it looked blue.

Mr. Brooks told me, "That's the north line."

My heart started beating faster. He told me how much money they wanted for it, and I said I would buy it and give him a ten thousand-dollar deposit right then and there. He informed me that the lady who was interested in buying it before I had come along was trying to come up with a down payment by Monday. He said if it didn't go through, he would call me that night and I could wire my deposit the next day.

I told him, "Please help me get this place."

I left and headed home. I prayed and said, "Lord, please help me buy this place. I fell in love with it as soon as I laid eyes on it."

I was restless all day Monday. I came home from work, and I asked Barbara if anyone had called. She told me no. We sat down to eat supper, and the phone rang. Mr. Brooks was calling to see if I still wanted the cattle ranch, and of course I told him yes.

"Wire me the ten thousand dollars in the morning, and I will get the papers rolling. It may take nine months to a year to get all the paperwork done."

"Whatever it takes, it will be fine. You don't have to worry about the final payment. I would write a check at closing."

I told my mom what I had done.

She asked, "Guilford, why do you want to own the world? I have never seen anyone like you."

I went to Western Union and wired the money. I went to work harder than ever. Mom was beginning to be excited about it. Shorty was doing a fine job at the shop. He was honest, and I gave him the key to the office and the gate so he could start opening and closing the shop. Barbara and Mom would come in to answer the phone and do paperwork. Mickey was doing a good job with the cattle. Kim was feeding the livestock. Mitchell and Corby were doing a great job with the roofing. Everything I touched turned out great.

I told Shorty that we were going to start selling parts for these old tractors, and I started buying tractors for the parts to resale. I was working every sale I could find all over North Carolina, Florida, and Alabama.

Shorty's oldest boy, Teinne, had grown up by this time, so I hired him to drive a truck for me, hauling equipment and tractors back to the auction yard. Mr. Brooks kept sending me papers on the land, and after about eleven months, we were nearly ready to close the deal.

Barbara and I left the kids with Mom and went to meet Mr. Brooks. I wrote the check. He made the deed out to us. The ranch was fenced for cattle. An old man named Hezekiah Ball lived on the road going to the ranch. I asked if I could hire him to look after the cattle for me. He had a boy and two girls. I told him I would pay him well. He told me yes.

The ranch had the biggest tobacco contract in Madison County. I asked if he would work it for me. Times were hard there, so he took the job. I told Mickey what kind of cattle to buy and instructed him to take them to the ranch. After two years, we had about five hundred cattle.

In July 1972, KC and I were reading in *Progressive Farmer* magazine about some Texas longhorn cows that were for sale in Henrietta, Texas. We called the telephone number and talked to a man who told us the price of a bull and a cow. We told him to pen them up and said we would leave on Friday and see him on Saturday. We did not take a trailer with us. I told KC we would buy one somewhere when we got there.

We stopped at a store in Henrietta and got some drinks. The man at the store told us how to get to the ranch and said, "You better fill up your truck with gas because it's forty miles to the cow ranch and there isn't another gas station on the way there."

We got there about 2:00 p.m. on Saturday after we turned off the highway on a dirt road. It was twenty miles to the place where he had the cows penned up. He said the ranch was four thousand acres. I had never seen so many Texas longhorn cows in my life. Everywhere you looked, there was a cow. We picked out the two we wanted and asked the man where we could go to buy a trailer to haul them back home.

He said, "The nearest place is one that builds trailers, and that's in Dallas, about sixty miles away."

We drove there and told the man what size trailer to build with a top on it. He gave us a price and said it would take about three or four days to build it. We gave him a deposit to start on the trailer and told him we would be back in four or five days.

I told KC, "Let's go to Mexico."

I had all my IDs from being in the service. KC didn't have anything. We went to a morgue in Dallas, and the man typed up a birth certificate for KC. The next day we went to the airport and bought a ticket to Old Mexico City. We hired a taxi driver that could speak English to drive us around for the next three days. He drove us out in the country to the slaughter pens where they kill cows and goats. That night he drove us to a nice steak house.

I looked at the menu and pointed to what I wanted to drink. I thought I had pointed to a tea on the rocks and assumed I was getting tea in ice. I said my blessing and started eating my food. I took two or three swallows of my "tea," but it was not tea. It was tequila on the rocks. I sure don't want any more of that. I talked to the taxi driver. He told the waitress what I wanted, and she got it.

The next day we went shopping and bought all kinds of clothes to bring home. They were people cooking all over town, chickens and all kinds of food. People were walking down the street with five and ten chickens in a string across their shoulders. I told KC that I sure didn't want any chicken. The flies were all over them. The next day we came back to Dallas, got our trailer and the cows, and came home.

Things began to turn bad for Mickey. His wife left him and moved back home to Baltimore. I asked what he was going to do, and he said he was going to stay with me. He loved me, and I loved him.

Mr. Ball's health was failing, and I needed to find someone to look after things, so I hired Pete Grainger. Never married and in his forties, he walked with a limp. He was already working with me in the roofing company. I fixed up the old house, and it was so nice. It had five bedrooms. I moved Kim, Mom, Robin, and Pete into the house.

Everything was rolling along. I took a tractor, mule, and a cutting horse that I bought Kim. He and Pete loved it. Mom wanted to bring some of her chickens too, so Barbara and I caught two crates full of chickens and carried them to Mom. We went every weekend unless I had to go look for roofing jobs.

Mickey told me one morning that he had met a man who wanted him to buy goats and pigs from him. His name was Lloyd Turner, and he was from Elizabeth City, North Carolina. I agreed. I had met the man about two years earlier in Georgia. We had a pen where we kept the goats, and he would deliver them once a week to Lloyd at the Rocky Mount Stockyard in North Carolina.

One day I was looking at the goats, and a man stopped on the side of the road. He introduced himself to me. His English wasn't really that good, but I could understand him. He said he was from Pakistan, which was part of India until the war and then India became a country. He wanted to buy a goat, so I sold him one.

Every three weeks he came back and bought

another goat. One day he came, and we talked for a while.

He told me, "I'm going back home to visit Pakistan in July. Would you like to visit my country?"

I said, "Let me think about it."

I had read the Bible and about how Moses had led the children of Israel out of Egypt. They were scattered all over the place, and I wanted to go and see for myself. I desired to see the Promised Land where Jesus was born. I wanted to trod on the path that Jesus had walked on.

I asked KC if he wanted to go with me, and he said yes. I had gotten all my shots when I was in the service, so all I needed was my passport. KC had to get his shots and his passport. When the Pakistani man came back, I told him we were going to visit his land. So when July came, we were ready. I had told all my people. They were to take care of everything until I got back, which would be about three weeks.

It came time to leave, and KC, the Pakistani man and his wife, and I loaded up in my car. We drove to JFK Airport in New York and boarded the plane. We landed in Paris first. We stayed there to board another plane, which would carry us to Karachi, Pakistan. From there, we rode a bus to Lyallpur, which was ninety miles of dirt roads.

I could not believe how the people were living. The shepherds were still tending their flocks, just like in the Bible. It was so amazing to read about it and then get to see it. It was like those days when the children of Israel came out of bondage. I had never seen so many flies in all my life, except in Mexico. Flies covered every fruit stand in the city. The goats, sheep, donkeys, and chickens were all over town. I couldn't believe that we had gone back that far in time.

We stayed there for two weeks and left. We caught a bus back to Karachi and stayed there overnight. The next day, we got on a plane to leave for Tel Aviv. We landed in Cairo to fuel up. They couldn't let us off the plane. There was fighting and bombs falling everywhere.

KC looked at me and said, "I told you we were going to be killed over here."

We left Cairo and landed in Tel Aviv. We took a taxi to Jerusalem and stayed in a motel room. The next day we found a taxi tour guide. When I was little, I had two curls in my hair, and Mom would say I would eat bread in many nations.

I thought, *Lord, it has come true.*

I always wanted to walk where Jesus had marched. The first place we went was Bethlehem, where Jesus was born. It was a long drive. When I walked into the manger, my eyes filled with tears because I was standing where my Savior was born. We left there and came back to Jerusalem. The next day we went to the Sea of Galilee and the Dead Sea. I waded in up to my knees and then returned to Jerusalem.

The next day, I told the guide I wanted to walk the path Jesus hiked to Golgotha Hill. As I walked that path, I couldn't explain how it felt, and when we came to the place where Jesus fell beneath the load of the cross, tears filled my eyes. I thought, *Lord, what a heavy load You bore, the sins of the whole world on Your shoulders.*

He was a man in the flesh like you and I, but He was also the Son of God. I remembered the prayer that he had uttered in the garden of Gethsemane. "If it could be your will, let this cup pass from me. Not my will, but thine will be done."

We went on to Golgotha Hill where they nailed Jesus and two thieves to crosses. The next day we went to the place where Abraham offered his son, Isaac, as a burnt offering to the Lord. They called it the Western Wall or the Wailing Wall. They said any person who laid his hand on the wall and uttered his prayer would have it come true.

I laid my hand on the wall and began to pray to God to bless my hands and take me home safe. The next day I told the guide I wanted to go to the tomb where they had laid Jesus. When we got there, the big stone was lying by the door. I had to bow down to go in. After I got in, I could stand up. I can't explain how it felt.

The next day the guide drove us back to Tel Aviv to catch a plane for our journey home. A lot of people were at the airport. Long lines of people were waiting to board the planes, and I was next to get on the plane. KC was behind me. They closed the gate. We had to wait for the next plane.

After we got on the plane and got settled, the

flight attendant came on over the speaker. The other plane had been hijacked. Later we found out that they had made the pilot fly into Beirut. We also heard that they had killed several people on the plane, mostly Americans. I guess I had cheated death again for the tenth time by the grace of God.

We flew back and saw Barbara and all the men who worked for me. I asked how things were going, and they said everything was fine. Shorty informed me that he needed help because the tractor parts were going quickly. I hired another man, Larry Holmes, also a mechanic.

Mickey said the cattle business was staying busy too. I got back on the road again and started buying farm equipment, parts, and tractors. I went back to working my auction business as usual. My life hasn't been the same since I took that trip. I looked at things differently.

Barbara and I went to the ranch to see how Mom and the kids were doing. Everything was fine. Pete met Mr. Ball's daughter, Jena, and he liked her very much. They stayed up there one more year until Robin, our daughter, was old enough to go to school.

Kim finished school, and I could tell they wanted to come home. I told them to be patient and said I would find someone who would move in and look after the place.

I started talking to some people in Marshall, looking for someone honest who could look after the cattle ranch when I brought my family home. I finally found Ed Edmond. I told him what I would pay him to work the place and look after the cattle. He agreed to it. I asked him to give me time to move my family out. Then he could move in.

It took about a month to get everything moved. Pete said he wanted to bring Jena with him. They wanted to get married, so I said that was fine. I moved everyone home, and Pete and Jena got married. He went back to work roofing. After about three years, they had a baby boy.

I had a big contract with the Boys and Girls Home at Lake Waccamaw to sheet and cover a large building that they had built. I went down to check on the job. Pete was pushing plywood up to the men on the roof. He told me his side was hurting. I asked if he wanted to go to the doctor. He said that he would be all right.

That night Pete died. A blood vessel had ruptured in his side, and he had bled to death. I sure hated to lose him.

We finished the job, and I got a contract to roof the Good Shepherd Home at Lake Waccamaw. The high-voltage electric wires were just three feet above the building. We had to be very careful.

One day I was on the job and picked up a piece of metal eve strip to give one of the men. I was holding it up, and one of the men hollered, "Guilford, look out!"

I was two feet from touching the wire. It would have killed me for sure. I cheated death again by the grace of God for the eleventh time.

Kim wanted to move back to the mountain ranch. I agreed and said he could look after the cattle and I would set him up with a roofing business up there. He was doing fine. I had set him up with Best Distributing, a roofing distributor, AKA Beacon Roofing, established in 1880. They deliver roofing materials to most roofing contractors all over the East Coast.

Everything was looking good. I was working the farm equipment sales all over the neighboring states.

I was in Dothan, Alabama, when Barbara called me on the sale yard. She told me that I needed to come home. Things with Kim were not going well, and they needed me.

So I came home. I moved him back home and got another man to work the farm. I tried to still work with Kim, but he was so rebellious. Then one day, I got a call while in Ocala, Florida. Barbara again told me that I needed to come home. Things were falling apart once more. Mickey had become somewhat rebellious as well.

I came home and told Kim that he was on his own. I had a long talk with Mickey. He promised me that he would straighten up, and he did for a while. Shorty and Larry were doing a good job with the tractors and parts yard.

I hired a lady to help Barbara with all the work in the office. I told her what to do about the roofing calls and said I would call her every day to check in. I informed Barbara that she could start going on the road with me. Robin was about grown. Barbara had done a wonderful job raising her. Shorty and his family loved her, and we loved their family as well.

Barbara and I went to a sale in Ocala. Teinne was hauling equipment and tractors daily. Barbara and I worked that sale and headed to another one in Tennessee. That night while I was driving, I looked in the rearview mirror and saw a car coming at a high rate of speed.

I said, "Oh Lord, he is going to hit us."

About that time, he pulled to the left and just did miss us. I started slowing down in anticipation for what could go wrong. He went across the median and ran into the front of an eighteen-wheeler. I stopped and went over there. He had gone through the truck. The cab of the truck was sitting on the side of the road. The driver was sitting in the seat.

I asked him, "Are you all right?"

"I think so."

I had a flashlight. I was looking around. Body parts were all over the road. The car was torn all to pieces. People began to gather around, and soon the road was blocked off. The state trooper got there. I told him what had happened, and we left. I guess I had cheated death again for the twelfth time by the grace of God.

We went on to Tennessee to work the sale the next day. Everything was fine. About three weeks later, I came home from a sale that I had gone to without Barbara. It was on a Thursday evening. She came to me to tell me that she had some bad news for me.

"What's wrong?"

"Someone called and said they found Bridget [my oldest daughter by my first wife] dead on the couch."

"Oh Lord!"

A man there had just finished pouring some concrete, and as I watched him, something spoke to me and said it wouldn't be but a few days before there would be another death. I told Barbara and the man.

They did an autopsy. She had overdosed on drugs. We went on Saturday to make funeral arrangements. Mickey went with us. We planned to bury her on Monday at 2:00 p.m. We stopped by the florist and bought the flowers. Mickey bought some too.

We got up Sunday morning and went to church. When we left church and went home, I told Barbara that I wanted to be alone for a while. I said I was going to Bladen County to the hunting woods. I stayed for about two hours and came home.

When I got to the house, Barbara was crying.

"What's wrong?" I asked.

"I tried to run you down and catch you."

"What's wrong?"

"They found Mickey dead in the bed around twelve thirty."

I thought my heart would burst. We sent him for an autopsy, and he had overdosed on morphine. Bridget was thirty-two; Mickey was forty-two. After we buried them, I called my associate in the cattle business and told them that I was closing it down. I had to walk on. I remembered my aunt's family when I was a little boy. She had two boys get killed in a fertilizer truck. I recall thinking about her pain and what she must have been feeling.

I continued to work with the equipment auction. Teinne was hauling, and Shorty and Larry were setting up the yard. We had a sale once a month. One day at Godley Auction in Charlotte, I met a man, Louie LeMay, from Waterboro, Maine. He had a tractor and parts business. I asked if he would start coming to my sales once a month, and he agreed.

The night before the next big sale we had, there was a big snow. The next morning, the equipment could not even be seen. We had to call off the sale. Louie came up and wanted to buy a load of tractors to take back. I told him of course. He was used to the snow.

We went out on the yard to find what he wanted. Shorty, Larry, and Teinne began loading the truck. I called Godley Auction and asked about his checks. They said they were good. We started doing a great load of business together with L & S Equipment. Sometimes we would load two tractor trailers full each month. The auction was doing great.

After about four months, Louie asked if I would like to ride with him and see his place. I told him yes. We would be back in about a week to get another load. So I got in, and we left. We got there the next day, and I saw several tractors that I had sold him.

I went into his shop, and he had two men working. One was taking tractors apart and putting parts in bins; the other was working on them to put them up for sale. I told him that his shop was very similar to mine. I got introduced to his mechanic, Harold Hall, who invited me to supper. Afterwards he took me to a motel downtown.

After three days, Louie told me that he was going to let Harold take me back home and he would get another load of tractors while there. After that we would trade over the phone.

After Harold and I got to know each other better and after doing business with Louie for about a year, I got to thinking about setting up a farm equipment business in his hometown of Maine. I drove up there one weekend and got a motel room.

I called Harold when I got there, and we met the next day. I asked how he would like for us to set up a yard and start the same kind of business. He said he would like that. I told him that I was going home in a couple of days and instructed him and his wife to think about it. I promised that I would be back in a week.

I rode around the next day looking at the land in the area. The next week I worked at the sales in Goldsboro at Wayne Equipment Company. I bought a big load of equipment. Teinne and I loaded it and went home that night. The next morning, we started unloading it all. One chain was left to hold the load. Teinne was running the loader, and a big six-foot and eight-foot cultivator was on there.

I walked to the side of the trailer to unlatch the chain binder. I took one step, and the cultivator fell over, missing me by a couple of inches. One half-second earlier and it would have fallen on me. It would have killed me for sure. I had cheated death for the thirteenth time by the grace of God. I thanked Him so much.

The next week, I called Harold and told him that I was coming to spend a week with him and to talk about the business opportunity, if he were still interested. He instructed me to come on. That week ended, and Barbara and I left for Waterboro. Harold told us that we could stay at his house.

I told him, "No thank you. We'll get a motel."

We had a meeting for two hours to discuss how we were going to set up the business. I told him to keep working until I found a place to buy. Barbara and I started riding the roads. We rode in and out four to five days. Later we rode down Route 202 for about twenty miles from Waterboro, and a sign said "forty acres for sale."

I stopped and got out. I walked over in the woods for a while. Barbara stayed in the car. It was a perfect site on a main road. I called the number on the sign, and it was a lawyer. I told him that I was interested in the land on highway 202. He instructed me on how to get to his office. We discussed the price, and I told him to let me talk to my partner. I said I would be back in touch with him the next day.

I called Harold and told him what I had found. We went to look at it. He said that it was a nice place and that he could take a dozer and clean what we needed as we went. I went to see the man the next day, and I told him that I would buy it.

I asked Harold for a good lawyer. He sent me to Mr. Knight, so Barbara and I went to his office. He called the other lawyer, and we argued a bit over the price. I left him a five thousand-dollar deposit and told him to try to get everything done within thirty days.

He told me that he would. I informed Harold that I had bought the land and to come with me and go to work driving a truck. I had an extra eighteen-wheeler with a drop-deck trailer that he could drive. He agreed. I told him when I got done with the paperwork, he could take the truck and trailer, bring the dozer off the yard, and start to work on the land. So I put him on the payroll.

When we got home, he stayed with me. He started to work on the truck and trailer, getting it safe for the road. The next week, there was a sale in Ocala. We loaded up and left that Sunday with the tractors. We worked the sale, sold the load, and bought another. We were reloading for a sale in Dothan, Alabama. We did it and went on to Bristol, Tennessee, on a Friday. We worked that sale and headed home.

I asked Harold how he liked the sale, and he told me that it was different, but he liked it. Teinne had come in with the load from Florida. He told Harold that he had surely taken a load off him. I informed him that Harold would only be there for two or three more weeks because I had bought a place in Maine and that Harold would be hauling up there and I would not be riding with him anymore.

I started driving and flying to the sales. We stayed

in contact by phone. Three weeks later, Mr. Knight called and said that all the paperwork was done. He asked how I wanted the deed. I said I would be there by the end of the week with a check.

I told Harold, "Load a D6 Cat dozer, and let's go to work clearing the land. I'm going this upcoming weekend. Get up with a good building contractor." I wanted to get the ball rolling so we could move into the shop by spring.

God was surely blessing my hands. Barbara and I drove back up that weekend. We got all the paperwork done. We went to the land and decided where to put the road and build the shop and office. I met with the building contractor, and we made a deal of what we wanted.

He drew up the plans and mailed them to me. I looked over them as well, along with the price of it. I sent them back to him. As soon as Harold got the road fixed where we were going to put the office and the shop, the contractor started on the building.

I went three weeks after that to look at everything, and it was coming along fine. I gave him a partial payment on the building. I told Harold to haul one load per week and keep it clean. In three months, the building was finished, and the yard looked good. I went back in six weeks, and Harold had already sold some tractors and equipment.

Mom got sick and died in March of that year. After we buried her, Teinne came to me and said he was tired of trucking. He had a chance to go work with a tire company. I agreed to let him go.

I started having others haul my equipment, and I liked that better because I didn't have to worry about having my trucks on the road. Robin was now grown and went to work for the local county government.

After about a year, Corby said he wanted to slow down and not work every day. I told him that I could handle that. After about three months, he quit entirely. I sold all my cattle on the mountain ranch and then the ranch.

I told Barbara, "I'm going to slow down.

"It's about time. You've been going most of our married life."

After about twenty years, Shorty got diabetes, and eight years later, he died. I had a lady, Vicky Long, helping Barbara. She would work just like a man. She filled in some of the gaps, and Larry was still with me.

One evening after supper, Barbara and I were sitting on the couch when the phone rang. It was Kim, my oldest son.

He was on dope bad. He said, "I need money."

"I am not buying your dope or financing you." I meant it.

"I'll be over to your house in a few minutes because I'm going to straighten you out."

"Come on. I'm home."

I got my double-barrel shotgun, and I set it by the couch. I thought he knew not to come kicking down my door. In a little while, he drove up, kicking the breezeway door. When he did, I shot both barrels through the door.

I missed him, and he ran out the other door. I sprinted after him. I had reloaded and shot at him again. It had hit the corner of the house. He had gone running down the road, and I reloaded again. I shot at him for a third time, and this time I got him. He had a butt full of bird shot.

He hollered, "I'm bleeding!"

"I can fix that." But I didn't shoot him anymore.

I went back to the house. He didn't come back to straighten his dad out anymore. A few years later, he shot and killed himself. It hurt me, but I thank God that I didn't kill him. His mother and sister had died, and now he was gone too. All I had left from him was his son Matthew, whom we called Matt.

My mind went back to Job in the Bible. He had lost it all. His wife told him to curse God and die. He told her that she talked like a foolish woman. Naked I came into the world, and naked I shall return. The Lord giveth, and the Lord taketh away. Blessed be the name of the Lord.

I had to get up and walk on again. I started working sales in my home state of North Carolina. I would be home every night. My brother-in-law Mitchell was still working in my roofing business.

About two years later, Corby fell dead. A year and a half later, Larry was found dead in his bed. Robin had gotten married and moved on with her life. Harold kept the business in Maine going well, and Barbara and I, along with Vicky, kept the tractors and parts business moving along. I kept cows on the farm, but not as many as I once had. I had quit the auction business due to not having any help.

I put in a set of heavy-duty scales and started buying scrap metal. This was something that we could do and stay home. People wanted or called to sell their tractors and equipment, so I began to stay home more. Harold would come down once a month and get a load, and I would drive up there about every six weeks. I hired Timmy Fowler to run a loader to load and unload scrap metal. My grandson Matt moved into my mom's old home place with his wife, Cathy, and their little boy. Matt had a welding business but helped me all he could. Everything went well for the next four years.

I finally told Barbara, "Let's sell the place in Maine. I'm tired of being on the road so much."

So we found a buyer and sold it.

The next year on July 18 at 5:35 p.m., my soul mate and the love of my life, Barbara, died. My whole world had caved in on me. Time had taken a toll on my life. I had to get up and walk on again. Life goes on. The Lord giveth, and the Lord taketh away. Blessed be the name of the Lord. The Lord gave her to me for a season. She was a beautiful flower. I can't bring her back, but I can go where she has gone.

Two years later, Timmy died. All the old bunch is gone on now. It's just Vicky and me left. We're still walking on. We keep the parts place going and wait for our day. This is the true story of my life. I know because I have lived it out by the grace of God, day by day.

To whoever may read this book, put God first in your life, for He is able to keep what is put into His hands. My dad put me into His hands when I was a little boy. I am eighty-one years old now and a living witness that God can and will take care of you.

Printed in the United States
By Bookmasters